Casserole Cookbook: A Hea with 50 Amazing Whole Fc Recipes That are Easy on

C000065163

by Vesela Tabakova
Text copyright(c)2016 Vesela Tabakova

Dedication
To my Mom and Dad - Thank You!

Table Of Contents

Easy Casserole Recipes That Are Actually Healthy   5
Mediterranean Chicken Casserole   6
Chicken and Potato Casserole   7
Easy Chicken Parmigiana   8
Mediterranean Chicken Drumstick Casserole   9
Greek Chicken Casserole   10
Hunter Style Chicken   11
Chicken with Almonds and Prunes   12
Sweet and Sour Sicilian Chicken   13
Moroccan Chicken Casserole   14
Chicken Moussaka   16
Chicken and Rice Casserole   18
One-Pot Chicken Dijonnaise   20
Blue Cheese and Mushroom Dump Chicken   22
Pesto Chicken   23
Greek Chicken And Lemon Rice   24
Spicy Chicken and Bean Stew   26
Mediterranean Beef Casserole   27
Mixed Vegetables with Beef   28
Ground Beef and Chickpea Casserole   30
Ground Beef and Rice Stuffed Peppers   31
Stuffed Tomatoes with Bulgur and Ground Beef   32
Stuffed Artichokes   34
Stuffed Cabbage Leaves with Ground Beef and Rice   35
Potato Moussaka   37
Eggplant Moussaka   39
Zucchini Moussaka   41
Homemade Lasagna   42
Beef and Spinach Lasagna   44
Baked Ground Beef Pasta   45
Sausage and Beans   47
Mediterranean Pork Casserole   48
Bulgarian Pork and Rice Casserole   49
Pork Roast and Cabbage   50
Orange Pork Chops   51
Pork Chops with Balsamic Roasted Vegetables   52

Mediterranean Lamb Casserole 54
Lamb and Potato Casserole 56
Mediterranean Baked Fish 57
Sea Bass Baked with Fennel 58
Ratatouille 59
Summer Pasta Bake 60
Homemade Baked Beans 61
Rice Stuffed Bell Peppers 62
Bean Stuffed Bell Peppers 63
Monastery Stew 64
Potatoes Baked in Milk 65
Potato and Zucchini Bake 66
New Potatoes with Herbs 67
Feta Cheese Stuffed Zucchinis 68
Mediterranean Vegetable Casserole 69
Baked Mediterranean Casserole with Tofu and Feta Cheese 70
Okra and Tomato Casserole 71
Zucchinis with Chickpeas and Rice 72
FREE BONUS RECIPES: 15 Heartwarming Slow Cooker Soup Recipes Inspired by the Mediterranean Diet 73
Mediterranean Chickpea Soup 74
French Vegetable Soup 75
Minted Pea Soup 76
Brown Lentil Soup 77
Moroccan Lentil Soup 78
Curried Lentil Soup 79
Simple Black Bean Soup 80
Bean and Pasta Soup 81
Heartwarming Split Pea Soup 82
Minestrone 83
Slow Cooker Summer Garden Soup 84
Crock Pot Tomato Basil Soup 85
Cheesy Cauliflower Soup 86
Creamy Artichoke Soup 87
Tomato Artichoke Soup 88

Easy Casserole Recipes
That Are Actually Healthy

In a world where food is full of frightening artificial additives and flavorings, there is one simple and easy way to adopt a healthier lifestyle - the more unprocessed and real food you eat, the better.

Casseroles and one pot stews are a great way to feed the family and save on the washing up. While it may look and sound difficult to cook real food at home, you will soon realize you can throw together a healthy casserole in the same amount of time you'd need to order a takeout. One-pot cooking is the easiest and stress-free way of preparing fast, yet healthy dinners for the family. When time is short and all you want is to spend more time with your family, prep one of these crowd-pleasing casseroles in minutes and let your oven do the rest of the work.

Nothing says comfort like a casserole. Several beautiful and healthy ingredients, combined in one baking pan, and you will have a quick weeknight supper or a delicious weekend dinner - it doesn't get any easier than that!

A casserole is comfort food at its best - a simple, crowd pleasing meal that only requires one dish for cooking. At the end of a busy day one-pot cooking is just what you need to prepare delicious family dinners which are sure to please everyone at the table and to become all time favorites.

Mediterranean Chicken Casserole

Serves 4

Ingredients:

4 chicken breast halves

1 big onion, sliced

1 red bell pepper, thinly sliced

2 cups tomato pasta sauce

1/2 cup black olives, pitted

1/2 green olives, pitted

1/3 cup Parmesan cheese

¼ cup chopped parsley

3 tbsp olive oil

Directions:

Heat the oil in a large, deep frying pan over medium-high heat. Cook chicken breasts, turning, for 4-5 minutes or until golden. Transfer to a casserole.

Sauté the onion and bell pepper, stirring, for 3-4 minutes, or until the onion has softened. Transfer to the casserole. Add pasta sauce and olives. Season with salt and pepper.

Bake in a preheated to 350 F for 30-35 minutes, stirring halfway through. Sprinkle with Parmesan cheese and parsley and bake for 3-4 minutes more.

Chicken and Potato Casserole

Serves 4

Ingredients:

4 skinless, boneless chicken breast halves

12 oz baby potatoes

1 onion, sliced

2 carrots, halved

1 red bell pepper, halved, deseeded, cut

1 zucchini, peeled and sliced

4 garlic cloves, thinly sliced

1 cup water

3 tbsp olive oil

1 tsp dried oregano

Directions:

Preheat the oven to 350 F. Heat oil in a non stick frying pan over medium heat. Cook half the chicken, turning occasionally, for 5 minutes, or until brown all over. Set aside. Repeat with remaining chicken.

Peel the potatoes and cut into quarters, lengthwise. Peel and cut the carrots and the zucchini. Cut the onion and the pepper.

Transfer chicken to an ovenproof dish and add the vegetables on and around the chicken. Add dried oregano, garlic, and water, distributing evenly across the pan.

Roast uncovered at 350 F for one hour. Halfway through stir gently. If needed, add a little more water.

Easy Chicken Parmigiana

Serves 4

Ingredients:

4 chicken breast fillets

1 eggplant, peeled and sliced lengthwise

1 can tomatoes, diced

9 oz mozzarella cheese, sliced

2 tbsp olive oil

Directions:

In an ovenproof casserole, heat olive oil and brown the chicken pieces.

Place eggplant over the chicken and add in tomatoes. Top with mozzarella slices and bake in a preheated to 350 F for 20 minutes or until cheese is golden.

Mediterranean Chicken Drumstick Casserole

Serves 4

Ingredients

8 chicken drumsticks

1 leek, trimmed, thinly sliced

2 garlic cloves, crushed

1 cup canned tomatoes

1 tsp dried rosemary

1 cup canned chickpeas, drained and rinsed

cooked orzo or couscous, to serve

Directions:

Preheat the oven to 350 F. Heat the oil in a non stick frying pan over medium heat. Add half the chicken and cook, turning occasionally, for 5 minutes, or until brown all over. Transfer chicken to a big baking dish. Repeat with the remaining chicken.

Add leek and garlic to the pan and cook, stirring, for 3 minutes or until soft. Add tomatoes, chickpeas, thyme and rosemary and bring to the boil. Remove from heat. Pour over the chicken.

Cover and bake for 40 minutes or until chicken is tender. Season with salt and pepper. Serve with orzo or couscous.

Greek Chicken Casserole

Serves 4

Ingredients:

4 skinless, boneless chicken breast halves or 8 tights

2 lb potatoes, cubed

1/2 lb green beans, trimmed and cut in 1 inch pieces

1 big onion, chopped

2 cups diced, canned tomatoes, undrained

5 cloves garlic, minced

1/4 cup water

1/2 cup feta cheese, crumbled

salt and black pepper, to taste

Directions:

Preheat oven to 350 F. Heat oil in a large baking dish over medium heat. Add onion and sauté for 2 minutes. Add thyme, black pepper and garlic and sauté for another minute. Add potatoes and sauté, for 2-3 minutes, or until they begin to brown. Stir in beans, water and tomatoes.

Remove from heat. Arrange chicken pieces into the vegetables, sprinkle with salt and pepper and top with feta. Cover and bake for 40 minutes, stirring gently halfway through. Serve the vegetable mixture on a plate underneath or beside the chicken.

Hunter Style Chicken

Serves 4-6

Ingredients:

1 chicken (3-4 lbs), cut into pieces

2 medium onions, thinly sliced

1 red bell pepper, cut

6-7 white mushrooms, sliced

2 cups canned tomatoes, diced and drained

3 garlic cloves, thinly sliced

2 tbsp olive oil

salt and freshly ground pepper

1/3 cup white wine

1/2 cup parsley leaves, finely cut

1 tsp sugar

Directions:

Rinse chicken pieces and pat dry. Heat olive oil in a large skillet on medium-high heat. Working in batches cook the chicken pieces until nicely browned, 5-6 minutes each side.

Transfer chicken to an ovenproof dish and set aside. In the same skillet, sauté the sliced onions and bell pepper for a few minutes. Add the mushrooms and cook some more until onion is translucent. Add garlic and cook a minute more.

Transfer vegetable mixture to the baking dish and add in wine, tomatoes and a teaspoon of sugar. Stir and bake for 40 minutes or until chicken is tender. Sprinkle with parsley, set aside for 3-4 minutes and serve.

Chicken with Almonds and Prunes

Serves 4

Ingredients:

1.5 lb chicken thigh fillets, trimmed

1/2 cup fresh orange juice

2 tbsp honey

1/3 cup white wine

1/2 cup pitted prunes

2 tbsp blanched almonds

2 tbsp raisins or sultanas

1 tsp ground cinnamon

salt and ground black pepper

1 tbsp fresh parsley leaves, chopped

couscous (to serve)

Directions:

Rinse chicken fillets and pat dry. Heat olive oil in a large skillet on medium heat. Working in batches cook the chicken pieces until nicely browned, 3-4 minutes each side. Transfer chicken to an ovenproof dish and set aside.

Combine orange juice, wine, honey, prunes, almonds, raisins and cinnamon in the same skillet. Bring to a boil, reduce heat to medium and boil for 5-8 minutes or until liquid is reduced by 1/3.

Pour over the chicken fillets and bake for 30 minutes, or until chicken is just tender. Season to taste with salt and pepper. Serve sprinkled with parsley and accompanied by couscous or orzo.

Sweet and Sour Sicilian Chicken

Serves 4

Ingredients:

4 chicken thigh fillets

1 large red onion, sliced

3 garlic cloves, chopped

2 tbsp flour

1/3 cup dry white wine

1 cup chicken broth

1/2 cup green olives

2 tbsp olive oil

2 bay leaves

1 tbsp fresh oregano leaves

2 tbsp brown sugar or honey

2 tbsp red wine vinegar

salt and black pepper, to taste

Directions:

Combine the flour with salt and black pepper and coat well all chicken pieces. Heat oil in ovenproof casserole and cook the chicken in batches, for 1-2 minutes each side, or until golden.

Add in onion, garlic, and wine and cook, stirring for 1 more minute. Add the chicken broth, olives, bay leaves, oregano, sugar and vinegar and bake, in a preheated to 380 F oven, for 20 minutes, or until the chicken is cooked through.

Moroccan Chicken Casserole

Serves 4-5

Ingredients:

1 whole chicken (3-4 lbs), cut into pieces

2 large onions, grated

2 or 3 cloves of garlic, finely chopped or pressed

1 tsp ginger

1 tsp cumin

1 tsp paprika

1 tsp black pepper

1 tsp tumeric

1/2 teaspoon salt

1/2 cup green or black olives, or mixed

1 preserved lemon, quartered and deseeded

5 tbsp olive oil

one bunch of fresh coriander

one bunch of fresh parsley

Directions:

Rinse and dry chicken and place onto a clean plate.

In a large bowl, mix three tablespoons of olive oil, salt, half the onions, garlic, ginger, cumin, paprika, and tumeric. Mix thoroughly, crush the garlic with your fingers, and add a little water to make a paste.

Roll the chicken pieces into that marinade and leave for 10 to 15 minutes.

Heat an ovenproof dish on medium heat and add 2 tablespoons of olive oil. Add in the chicken and marinade juices together with the remaining onions, olives and chopped preserved lemon.

Tie the parsley and coriander together into a bouquet and place on top of the chicken. Bake in a preheated to 350 F oven for 45 minutes or until the chicken is cooked through and quite tender. Serve with couscous, rice or rice pilaf.

Chicken Moussaka

Serves 6

Ingredients:

2 big eggplants, cut into 1/2 inch thick rounds

olive oil cooking spray

1 tbsp salt

1 big onion, chopped

1/2 tsp ground cinnamon

1/2 tsp ground nutmeg

1/4 tsp ground coriander

1/4 tsp ground ginger

2 cups canned tomatoes, undrained, chopped

2 cups skinless, shredded, roast chicken

1/2 cup finely chopped fresh parsley leaves

1 tsp sugar

1 cup yogurt

1 cup Parmesan cheese

salt and black pepper to taste

Directions:

Place eggplant slices on a tray and sprinkle with plenty of salt. Let sit for 30 minutes, then rinse with cold water. Lay slices out flat and use a clean kitchen towel to squeeze out excess water and pat dry.

Heat a frying pan over medium high heat. Spray both sides of eggplant with oil. Cook in batches for 3 to 4 minutes each side or until golden. Transfer to a plate.

In the same pan sauté onion, stirring, for 3 to 4 minutes or until softened. Add spice. Sauté for one minute until fragrant. Add tomatoes and sugar, stir and sauté until thickened. Add chicken and parsley and stir well to combine.

Arrange half the eggplant slices in a casserole. Cover with chicken and tomato mixture and arrange remaining eggplant. Top with yogurt and sprinkle with Parmesan cheese. Bake for 30 minutes or until golden. Set aside for five minutes and serve.

Chicken and Rice Casserole

Serves 6

Ingredients:

1 chicken 2-3 lbs, cut into serving pieces, or 2-3 lbs chicken thighs or breasts, rinsed and patted dry

5 tablespoons olive oil

1 medium onion, chopped

1 carrot, chopped

1 garlic clove, minced

1 1/2 cups white rice

2 cups chicken broth

1 cup water

1 cup of diced fresh or cooked tomatoes, strained

1 tsp savory

1 tsp salt

freshly ground black pepper, to taste

Directions:

Heat 3 tablespoons of olive oil in a large skillet on medium-high heat. Cook chicken pieces a for a few minutes on each side, enough to seal them. Remove from pan and set aside.

In the same pan, heat the remaining olive oil and sauté the onions, garlic and carrot for 2-3 minutes. Add the rice and cook, stirring until it becomes transparent.

Transfer rice mixture to an ovenproof baking dish. Pour over the chicken broth, tomatoes and water. Stir until well combined. Arrange chicken pieces on top, skin side up, and bake in a preheated to 350 F oven for 45 minutes until the rice and chicken are done.

One-Pot Chicken Dijonnaise

Serves 4

Ingredients:

4 chicken breasts with skin

1 onion, sliced

5-6 white button mushrooms, sliced

2 garlic cloves, crushed

1 tbsp flour

1/3 cup Dijon mustard

1/3 cup mayonnaise

1/3 cup dry white wine

1/3 cup chicken broth

1/2 cup sour cream

2 tbsp olive oil

2 tbsp finely chopped tarragon

salt and pepper, to taste

Directions:

Heat oil in an ovenproof casserole over medium heat. Cook chicken in batches for 2-3 minutes each side until golden. Add onion and sauté for 3 more minutes or until soft.

Stir in the mushrooms and garlic and cook, stirring, for a further minute. Add in flour and stir to combine. Add wine, mayonnaise, Dijon mustard, chicken broth and tarragon and combine well.

Cover with a lid or foil and bake in a preheated to 380 F oven for 10-15 minutes or until chicken is cooked through and the liquid has evaporated. Add in sour cream, salt and black pepper to taste and heat through.

Blue Cheese and Mushroom Dump Chicken

Serves 4

Ingredients:

4 chicken breast halves

6-7 white button mushrooms, sliced

1 cup crumbled blue cheese

1/2 cup sour cream

salt and black pepper, to taste

1 cup walnuts, crushed, to serve

Directions:

Heat oven to 350 degrees F. Spray a casserole with non stick spray. Place all ingredients into it, turn chicken to coat.

Bake for 35-40 minutes or until chicken juices run clear. Sprinkle with walnuts and serve.

Pesto Chicken

Serves 4

Ingredients:

5-6 chicken breast halves

1 small jar pesto sauce

1 cup sour cream

Directions:

In a bowl, combine pesto and sour cream.

Heat oven to 350 degrees F. Spray a casserole with non stick spray. Place chicken and pesto mixture into it, turn chicken to coat.

Bake for 35-40 minutes or until chicken juices run clear.

Greek Chicken And Lemon Rice

Serves 4

Ingredients:

4 chicken thighs, skin on, bone in

1 small onion, finely cut

1 garlic clove, minced

1 cup white rice

11/2 cups water

3 tbsp olive oil

1 tsp salt

black pepper, to taste

for the marinade:

2 lemons, juiced

2 tbsp lemon zest

1 tbsp dried oregano

4 garlic cloves, minced

1 tsp salt

Directions:

Combine the chicken and marinade ingredients in a bowl and set aside for at least 30 minutes.

Heat olive oil in an ovenproof casserole dish on medium-high heat. Remove chicken from marinade, but reserve the marinade. Cook chicken pieces for a few minutes on each side, enough to seal them.

Add in onions, garlic, rice and reserved marinade and stir to combine.

Stir in water, season with salt and pepper to taste, and bake in a preheated to 350 F oven for 30-35 minutes or until the rice and chicken are done.

Spicy Chicken and Bean Stew

Serves 4

Ingredients:

4 chicken thighs, skin on, bone in

1 small onion, finely cut

1 garlic clove, minced

2 red chillies, deseeded and chopped

1 can tomatoes, diced and undrained

2 cans kidney beans, drained

1 cup hot chicken broth

3 tbsp olive oil

1 tsp hot paprika

1 tsp salt

black pepper, to taste

1/2 cup fresh parsley, finely cut, to serve

1 cup sour cream

Directions:

Heat the olive oil in an ovenproof casserole dish on medium-high heat. Cook chicken for a few minutes on each side, until brown all over.

Add in onions, garlic, chillies and hot paprika and stir to combine.

Stir in chicken broth, beans and tomatoes, season with salt and pepper to taste, cover, and cook until the chicken is cooked through and tender.

Stir through the parsley and serve with sour cream.

Mediterranean Beef Casserole

Serves 6

Ingredients:

2 lb lean steak, cut into large pieces

3 onions, sliced

4 garlic cloves, cut

2 red peppers, cut

1 green pepper, cut

1 zucchini, cut

3 tomatoes, quartered

2 tbsp tomato paste or purée

1/2 cup green olives, pitted

1/2 cup dry red wine

1/2 cup of water

1 tsp dry oregano

salt and black pepper, to taste

Directions:

Heat olive oil in a deep ovenproof casserole and seal the beef. Add vegetables and stir.

Dilute the tomato paste in half a cup of water and pour it over the meat mixture together with the wine. Season well and bake, stirring halfway through, in a preheated to 350 F for one hour.

Mixed Vegetables with Beef

Serves 6-8

Ingredients:

2 lbs stewing beef

2 eggplants, peeled and cubed

5 small potatoes, peeled and halved

1 zucchini, peeled and cubed

2 red peppers, cut

1 cup frozen okra

1 onion, sliced

4 garlic cloves, cut

3 tomatoes, diced

1 cup parsley leaves, chopped

1/4 cup olive oil

1 tsp paprika

salt, to taste

black pepper, to taste

Directions:

Sprinkle the eggplant pieces with salt and set aside in a strainer for 15 minutes. Wash the salt and the excess juices and pat dry the eggplant pieces.

Heat the olive oil in a large pot and sauté the beef pieces for a few minutes until well browned. Add in the vegetables, stirring continuously. Add paprika, salt and pepper and stir again. Transfer the meat and vegetables to an ovenproof dish, cover with foil, and bake in a preheated to 305 F oven for an hour and a half. Sprinkle with parsley and serve.

Ground Beef and Chickpea Casserole

Serves 6

Ingredients:

1 lb ground beef

1 onion, chopped

2 garlic cloves, crushed

1 can chickpeas, drained

1 can sweet corn, drained

1 can tomato sauce

1/2 cup water

2 bay leaves

1 tsp dried oregano

1/2 tsp salt

1/2 tsp cumin

3 tbsp olive oil

black pepper, to taste

Directions:

Heat the olive oil in a casserole over medium-high heat. Add the onion and sauté for 4-5 minutes. Add garlic and sauté a minute more. Add in the ground beef and cook for 5 minutes, stirring, until browned.

Add the cumin and bay leaves, the tomatoes, corn and chickpeas. Bake in a preheated to 350 F for 20 minutes, or until the beef is cooked through. Remove the bay leaves and serve over pilaf or couscous.

Ground Beef and Rice Stuffed Peppers

Serves 6

Ingredients:

8 red or green bell peppers, cored and seeded

2 lbs ground beef

1/4 cup rice, washed and drained

1 onion, finely cut

1 tomato, grated

a bunch of fresh parsley, chopped

3 tbsp olive oil

1 tbsp paprika

Directions:

Heat the oil and gently sauté the onion for 2-3 minutes. Remove from heat. Add paprika, ground beef, rice and tomato and season with salt and pepper. Combine all ingredients very well and stuff each pepper with the mixture using a spoon. Every pepper should be 3/4 full.

Arrange the peppers in a deep ovenproof dish and top up with warm water to half fill the dish. Cover with a lid or foil and bake for about 40 minutes at 350 F. Uncover and bake for 5 minutes more. Serve with yogurt.

Stuffed Tomatoes with Bulgur and Ground Beef

Serves 6

Ingredients:

1 lb ground beef

6 large tomatoes

2 tbsp tomato paste or purée

1/2 cup bulgur

1 onion, shredded

2 garlic cloves, crushed

6 tsp sugar

1 tsp paprika

1 tsp mint

1/2 cup parsley leaves, finely cut

5 tbsp olive oil

salt and pepper to taste

2/3 cup Parmesan cheese, grated

Directions:

Slice the tops of the tomatoes in such a way as to be able to stuff the tomato and cover with the cap. With the help of a spoon, scoop out the tomato flesh and reserve in a bowl. Sprinkle a teaspoon of sugar in each tomato to help reduce the acidity.

Heat the olive oil in a large skillet and brown the ground beef. Add the onions and garlic and cook until transparent. Add the bulgur, parsley, finely cut tomato pulp and tomato paste. Season with paprika, mint, salt and pepper. Bring to the boil, then reduce heat and simmer for 5 minutes.

Drizzle some olive oil in the bottom of an ovenproof dish. Arrange the tomatoes in the dish. Stuff them with the meat mixture - each tomato should be about 3/4 full. Sprinkle with Parmesan cheese and bake in a preheated to 350 F oven for 30 minutes.

Stuffed Artichokes

Serves 6

Ingredients:

1 lb lean ground beef

1/3 cup rice, washed and drained

6 large firm fresh artichokes

1 onion, grated

2 garlic cloves, chopped

4 tomatoes, grated

5 tbsp olive oil

1/2 cup parsley leaves, very finely cut

1 tsp paprika

salt and pepper, to taste

juice of 1/2 lemon

Directions:

Peel artichokes and cut off tips. With the help of a spoon, carve out the center of artichokes. Put artichokes in a large bowl together with a tbsp of salt, lemon juice and enough water to cover them completely.

Heat olive oil in a cooking pot and sauté onions and garlic until transparent. Add in ground beef, rice, parsley and paprika. Cook for 5 min, stirring. Add tomatoes and cook until almost all liquid evaporates. Season with salt and pepper and remove from heat.

Wash and drain artichokes. Stuff artichokes with the already cooled mixture and arrange them in a casserole in one layer. Add 2 cups water bake ina preheated to 350 F for about 40 minutes.

Stuffed Cabbage Leaves with Ground Beef and Rice

Serves 8

Ingredients:

1 lb ground beef

20-30 medium sized pickled cabbage leaves

1 onion, diced

1 leek, finely cut

1/2 cup white rice

2 tsp tomato paste

2 tsp paprika

1 tsp dried mint

½ tsp black pepper

1/3 cup olive oil

salt to taste

Directions:

Sauté the onion and leek in the oil for about 2-3 minutes. Remove from heat and add the beef, tomato paste, paprika, mint, black pepper and the washed and drained rice. Add salt only if the cabbage leaves are not too salty. Mix everything very well.

In a large casserole, place a few cabbage leaves on the base. Place a cabbage leaf on a large plate with the thickest part closest to you. Spoon 1-2 teaspoons of the meat mixture and fold over each edge to create a tight sausage-like parcel.

Place in the casserole in one or two layers. Pour over some boiling water so that the water level remains lower than the top layer of cabbage leaves. Cover with foil and bake for around 40 minutes in a preheated to 350 F oven. Uncover and bake for 5 minutes more.

Potato Moussaka

Serves 4

Ingredients:

1 lb ground beef

1 celery rib, finely chopped

1 carrot, peeled, finely chopped

1 onion, finely chopped

2 garlic cloves, crushed

1 cup canned tomatoes, drained, diced

5 potatoes, peeled and cut into 1/4 inch cubes

1/2 cup fresh parsley leaves, finely cut

3 tbsp olive oil

1 tbsp summer savory or dried oregano

1 tsp paprika

2/3 cup yogurt

1 egg, lightly beaten

salt and freshly ground black pepper, to taste

Directions:

Heat half the oil in a large frying pan over medium-high heat. Add the ground meat and cook, stirring, using a spoon to break up lumps, for 5 minutes or until it changes color. Transfer to a large baking dish.

Heat the remaining oil in the same pan. Add the carrot, onion, garlic, parsley, paprika and savory and sauté, stirring, for 10 minutes, or until vegetables soften. Transfer to the baking dish and mix well with ground meat.

Wash, peel, and cut into small 1/4 inch cubes the potatoes. Stir potatoes into the meat and the vegetable mixture. Combine very well, add 1/2 cup of water, stir again and bake in a preheated to 350 F oven for 30 minutes, or until potatoes are cooked through. In a small bowl, mix together the yogurt and egg, pour and spread it evenly over the Moussaka. Bake for 5 more minutes or until golden. Set aside for five minutes and serve with a dollop of yogurt.

Eggplant Moussaka

Serves 6

Ingredients:

1 1/2 lbs ground beef

3 eggplants, peeled and cut into 1/2 inch thick rounds

1 big onion, chopped

1/2 tsp ground cinnamon

1/4 tsp ground coriander

1/2 cup canned tomatoes, undrained, chopped

1/2 cup parsley leaves, finely chopped

4 tbsp olive oil

1 tsp sugar

1 tsp salt

2/3 cup yogurt

1 egg

1 cup Parmesan cheese

salt and black pepper to taste

Directions:

Place eggplant rounds on a tray and sprinkle with plenty of salt. Let sit for 30 minutes, then rinse with cold water. Squeeze out excess water and pat dry.

Heat oil in a frying pan over medium high heat. Cook eggplant, in batches, for 3 to 4 minutes each side, or until golden. Transfer to a plate.

In the same pan sauté onion, stirring, for 3 to 4 minutes, or until softened. Add spice and sauté for one more minute until fragrant. Add ground beef, garlic, sugar and tomatoes. Stir and cook until the meat is no longer pink.

Arrange half the eggplant slices in a baking dish. Cover with meat mixture and arrange remaining eggplant. Bake in a preheated to 350 F oven for 30 minutes. In a small bowl mix together the yogurt, egg, and Parmesan cheese, pour and spread it evenly over the Moussaka. Bake for 5 more minutes, or until golden. Set aside for five minutes and serve.

Zucchini Moussaka

Serves 4

Ingredients:

1 lb ground beef

5 zucchinis, sliced

1/3 cup rice

3-4 garlic cloves, sliced

1 large onion, chopped

1/2 cup canned tomatoes

1/2 cup fresh dill, finely cut

2/3 cup yogurt

1 egg, lightly beaten

4 tbsp olive oil

1 tsp paprika

salt and black pepper, to taste

Directions:

Sauté the onions and garlic for a minute or two, stirring. Add the ground beef and cook it for 10 minutes until it is no longer pink. Add tomatoes, paprika, rice and dill and stir. Arrange half the zucchini slices in a baking pan. Spread ground beef mixture over them. Arrange the remaining zucchinis on top. Bake in a preheated to 350 F oven for 30 minutes.

In a small bowl, mix together the yogurt and egg, pour and spread it evenly over the Zucchini Moussaka. Bake for 5 more minutes, or until golden. Set aside for five minutes and serve.

Homemade Lasagna

Serves 9-10

Ingredients:

1.5 lbs lean ground beef

10 oz pancetta or bacon, cut into 1/4-inch pieces

1 onion, finely chopped

2 carrots, chopped

2 celery ribs, chopped

3 garlic cloves, crushed

1/2 cup dry white wine

1/2 cup chicken broth

2 cups canned tomatoes, diced

3 tbsp tomato paste

1 tbsp dried basil

1/3 cup parsley

1/2 tsp ground black pepper

1/4 tsp salt

1 tsp paprika

2 cups mozzarella cheese, shredded

1 cup Parmesan cheese, shredded

12 no-boil lasagna noodles

Directions:

Heat olive oil in a large pot and cook ground beef, pancetta, onion, carrots, celery, and garlic over medium-high heat until ground meat turns brown. Bring to a simmer and cook, uncovered, until liquid is nearly evaporated. Stir in wine and beef broth and continue simmering until liquid evaporates. Add in paprika, tomatoes, tomato paste, parsley, black pepper and salt.

Combine mozzarella and Parmesan cheese in a medium bowl.

Spread one-third of the meat sauce over the bottom of an ungreased 13x9x2-inch baking dish. Cover with one-fourth of the cheese mixture. Layer noodles. Repeat layering meat sauce, cheese mixture, and noodles two more times.

Cover dish with foil and bake in a preheated to 350 F oven for 40 minutes. Sprinkle with remaining cheese mixture and bake, uncovered, about 5 more minutes until the cheese turns gold. Set aside for 10 minutes and serve.

Beef and Spinach Lasagna

Serves 8-10

Ingredients:

1 lb lean ground beef

10 oz frozen spinach

1 onion, chopped

2 cups canned tomatoes

4 garlic cloves, crushed

1 tsp dried basil

1 tsp dried oregano

2 cups ricotta cheese

2 cups mozzarella cheese, shredded

12 no-cook lasagna noodles

Directions:

In a large skillet, sauté onion for a few minutes. Add beef and cook over medium heat until meat is no longer pink. Add in the tomatoes, garlic, basil and oregano. Simmer for 10 minutes. In a large bowl, combine the thawed spinach with half the ricotta and mozzarella cheese.

Spread one-third of the meat sauce over the bottom of an ungreased 13x9x2-inch baking dish. Sprinkle with one-fourth of the spinach -cheese mixture. Top with noodles. Repeat layering meat sauce, spinach mixture, and noodles two more times.

Cover dish with foil. Bake for 40 minutes in a preheated to 350 F oven. Sprinkle with the remaining cheese mixture. Bake, uncovered, about 5 minutes until cheese turns golden. Let stand for at least 10 minutes before serving.

Baked Ground Beef Pasta

Serves 6

Ingredients:

2 cups large pasta

1 lb ground beef

2 onions, finely chopped

4 garlic cloves, chopped

3-4 mushrooms, chopped

5-6 pickled gherkins, chopped

1 cup canned tomatoes, drained

1 tsp paprika

1 tsp dry basil

salt and black pepper, to taste

1/2 cup parsley leaves, chopped

1 cup mozzarella cheese, grated

1 egg, whisked

Directions:

Prepare pasta according to package directions. Drain and place in an oven proof dish.

Heat olive oil in a large pot and sauté onion until transparent. Add ground beef, mushrooms, garlic and tomatoes, stir and cook on low heat for about 15 minutes. When the meat is almost done, add the gherkins, the parsley and toss everything with the pasta.

Whisk the egg with mozzarella cheese and spread all over the pasta equally. Bake in a preheated to 350 F oven for 10 minutes or until the cheese turns golden.

Sausage and Beans

Serves 4

Ingredients:

1.7 lb lean beef sausages

1 big onion, thinly sliced

2 garlic cloves, crushed

2 cups canned white beans, drained, rinsed

1 cup canned tomatoes, drained, diced

1 tsp paprika

1 tbsp mint

1 tbsp sunflower oil

1/2 cup finely cut parsley, to serve

Directions:

Heat a non-stick frying pan over medium heat. Cook sausages for 8-10 minutes or until browned. Set aside to cool slightly the transfer to a board and cut.

Heat oil in a casserole and gently sauté onions, garlic and paprika for 3-4 minutes or until onion is soft. Add beans, tomatoes and mint. Stir. Add in sausages.

Bake in a preheated to 350 F oven for 15 minutes or until sauce is thick. Serve into bowls sprinkled with fresh parsley.

Mediterranean Pork Casserole

Serves 4

Ingredients:

1 1/2lb pork loin, cut into cubes

1 large onion, chopped

1 cup mushrooms, cut

½ cup chicken broth

2 garlic cloves, finely chopped

1 green pepper, deseeded and cut into strips

1 red pepper, deseeded and cut into strips

1 tomato, chopped

2 tsp olive oil

1 tsp savory

1 tsp paprika

salt and black pepper, to taste

Directions:

Add the olive oil to a casserole dish and seal the pork cubes for about 5 minutes, stirring continuously. Lower the heat, add the onion and garlic and sauté for 3-4 minutes until the onion is soft.

Add the paprika and savory and season with salt and pepper to taste. Stir in the peppers, tomato, chicken broth and mushrooms. Cover with foil and bake for 1 hour at 350 F, or until the pork is tender. Uncover and bake for 5 minutes more. Serve with boiled potatoes.

Bulgarian Pork and Rice Casserole

Serves 4

Ingredients:

1.5 lb pork cubed (leg or neck)

1 onion, cut

2 cups rice, washed

5 cups water

4 tbsp olive oil

1/2 cup finely cut parsley leaves, to serve

Directions:

Cut pork into pieces - approximately 2x1.2 inch. Heat two tablespoons of oil in a large, deep, frying pan over medium-high heat. Cook pork, turning, for 4-5 minutes, or until browned. Transfer to an ovenproof baking dish.

In the same pan, heat the remaining oil and sauté onion for 2-3 minutes. Add washed and drained rice and cook for 2-3 minutes, stirring continuously, until transparent. Transfer to the baking dish. Add 5 cups of warm water, stir well and bake in a preheated to 350 F oven for 40 minutes, stirring halfway through. When ready, sprinkle with parsley, set aside for 2-3 minutes and serve.

Pork Roast and Cabbage

Serves 4

Ingredients:

2 cups cooked pork roast, chopped

1/2 head cabbage

1 onion, chopped

1 lemon, juice only

1 tomato, chopped

2 tbsp olive oil

1 tsp paprika

1/2 tsp cumin

black pepper, to taste

Directions:

In an ovenproof casserole dish, heat olive oil and gently sauté cabbage, pork and onions. Add in cumin, paprika, lemon juice, tomato and stir. Cover, and bake at 350 F for 20-25 minutes, or until vegetables are tender.

Orange Pork Chops

Serves 4

Ingredients:

4 pork chops, about 4 oz each

1 onion, thinly sliced

4 garlic cloves, crushed

3 tbsp olive oil

1/4 tsp cumin

1/2 tsp dried oregano

1 tsp black pepper

1 tbsp raw honey

1 cup orange juice

Directions:

Crush the garlic, oregano, black pepper and cumin together into a paste. Rub each chop with the garlic paste and arrange them in a casserole dish.

Dilute one tablespoon of honey into the orange juice and pour it over the chops. Add in onions, stir, and bake in a preheated to 350 F on for 30 minutes, or until the chops are cooked through.

Pork Chops with Balsamic Roasted Vegetables

Serves 4

Ingredients:

4 pork chops

12 oz small red potatoes, halved

8 oz cremini mushrooms, halved

3-4 carrots, cut into sticks

1 medium red onion, cut into wedges

1 tsp thyme

1/2 tsp ground cumin

4 tbsp olive oil

1 tsp tomato paste

1/3 cup chicken broth

1 tbsp honey

3 tbsp balsamic vinegar

1/2 cup Gorgonzola cheese, crumbled

salt and black pepper, to taste

Directions:

Heat olive oil in an ovenproof casserole and cook pork chops 3 minutes on each side or until browned. Add the potatoes, carrots, onion and mushrooms. Season with salt and pepper, sprinkle with thyme and cumin.

In a bowl, combine tomato paste, balsamic vinegar, honey and chicken broth. Pour this mixture over the pork chops and vegetables. Cover and bake in a preheated to 420 F on for 30 minutes, stirring halfway through.

Mediterranean Lamb Casserole

Serves 5

Ingredients:

1 1/2 lb boned lean shoulder of lamb

3 onions, sliced

2 garlic cloves, chopped

1 cup canned chickpeas, drained and rinsed

2 zucchinis, cubed

1 cup cherry tomatoes, halved

1 cup beef broth

1 cup tomato juice

3 tbsp olive oil

1 tbsp flour

1 tbsp chopped fresh rosemary

1 tbsp fresh basil, chopped

1/3 tsp black pepper

½ cup fresh parsley leaves, to serve

Directions:

Cut the lamb into 1 inch cubes. In an ovenproof casserole, heat 2 tablespoons of the olive oil and gently sauté onions and garlic for about 2-3 minutes. Add the lamb and sauté, stirring, for about 4 minutes or until well browned on all sides. Add the flour and rosemary and stir.

Add the tomato juice and beef broth and bake in a preheated to 350 F for 1 hour. Stir in the chickpeas and bake for a further 1 hour or until the lamb is almost tender. Stir in courgettes, tomatoes, black pepper and basil. Cook for about 20 minutes longer or until the lamb is tender. Serve sprinkled with parsley.

Lamb and Potato Casserole

Serves 6

Ingredients:

1 1/2 pounds shoulder lamb chops

12 small new potatoes, peeled, whole

3 large onions, sliced

2 carrots, sliced

2 tbsp olive oil

2 tsp dried parsley

2 tsp dried mint

1/2 tsp pepper

1/2 tsp salt

Directions:

Place lamb chops into a greased casserole dish. Cover them with sliced onion, carrots, parsley, salt and pepper. Arrange new potatoes on and around the meat. Add enough cold water to fill the dish halfway.

Bake, covered with foil, for 45 minutes in a preheated oven. Remove the foil and bake for 30 minutes more.

Mediterranean Baked Fish

Serves 4

Ingredients:

1 ½ flounder or sole fillets

3 tomatoes, chopped

1/2 onion, chopped

2 cloves garlic, chopped

1/3 cup white wine

20 black olives, pitted and chopped

1 tbsp capers

3 tbsp olive oil

1 tbsp fresh lemon juice

1 tsp dry oregano

4 leaves fresh basil, chopped

3 tbsp Parmesan cheese

Directions:

Preheat oven to 350 F. Heat olive oil in an ovenproof casserole and sauté onion until translucent. Add in garlic, oregano and tomatoes. Stir and cook for 4-5 minutes.

Add wine, olives, capers, lemon juice and the chopped basil. Blend in Parmesan cheese, and arrange fish in this sauce. Bake for 20 minutes in the preheated oven, until fish is easily flaked with a fork.

Sea Bass Baked with Fennel

Serves 4

Ingredients:

4 skinned sea bass fillets, 4½ oz each

5 oz fennel, trimmed and sliced

½ cup dry white wine

a bunch of green onions, chopped

10 black olives, pitted and halved

salt and black pepper, to taste

1 tbsp lemon zest

1 tbsp capers

2 garlic cloves, finely chopped

½ tsp paprika

salt and pepper, to taste

Directions:

Arrange the sliced fennel in a shallow ovenproof casserole. Add the green onions and lay the fish on top. Season with salt and pepper to taste. Scatter the capers, garlic, olives, paprika and lemon zest over the fish, then pour the wine over the top.

Cover the dish with foil and bake for 30 minutes, or until the fish flakes easily.

Ratatouille

Serves 4

Ingredients:

1 eggplant, cut into small cubes

2 large tomatoes, chopped

2 zucchinis, sliced

1 onion, sliced into rings

1 green pepper, sliced

150g sliced fresh mushrooms

3 cloves garlic, crushed

2 tsp dried parsley

½ cup Parmesan cheese

3 tablespoons olive oil

Directions:

Place eggplant pieces on a tray and sprinkle with plenty of salt. Let sit for 30 minutes, then rinse with cold water.

Heat olive oil in an ovenproof casserole over medium heat. Gently sauté garlic for a minute or two. Add in parsley and eggplant. Continue sautéing until eggplant is soft. Sprinkle with a tablespoon of Parmesan cheese.

Spread zucchinis in an even layer over the eggplant. Sprinkle with a little more cheese. Continue layering onion, mushrooms, pepper and tomatoes, covering each layer with a sprinkling of Parmesan cheese. Bake in a preheated to 350 F oven for 40 minutes.

Summer Pasta Bake

Serves 4

Ingredients:

1 small eggplant, cubed

2 zucchinis, cubed

1 red onion, sliced

3 cloves garlic, crushed

1 green pepper, chopped

3 tomatoes, diced

4 tablespoons olive oil

sea salt and freshly ground black pepper to taste

1 tsp dried oregano

1 cup uncooked penne pasta

½ cup feta cheese, crumbled

Directions:

Place eggplant slices on a tray and sprinkle with plenty of salt. Let sit for 30 minutes, then rinse with cold water.

Combine all vegetables in a large baking dish. Add in olive oil, salt, pepper and oregano. Toss to coat the vegetables well. Bake in a preheated to 350 F oven until the vegetables are very soft.

Boil the pasta according to package directions. Drain and toss with the baked vegetables. Add cheese and toss to combine again. Season to taste with salt and black pepper and serve.

Homemade Baked Beans

Serves 6

Ingredients:

2 cups dried white beans

2 medium onions, chopped

1 red bell pepper, chopped

1 carrot, chopped

1/4 cup sunflower oil

1 tsp paprika

1 tsp black pepper

1 tbsp plain flour

1/2 bunch fresh parsley and mint

1 tsp salt

Directions:

Wash the beans and soak in water overnight. In the morning discard the water, pour enough cold water to cover the beans, add one of the onions, peeled but left whole. Cook until the beans are soft but not falling apart. If there is too much water left, drain the beans.

Chop the other onion and fry it a frying pan along with the chopped bell pepper and the carrot. Add paprika, plain flour and the beans. Stir well and pour the mixture in a baking dish along with some parsley, mint, and salt. Bake in a preheated to 350 F oven for 20-30 minutes. The beans should not be too dry. Serve warm.

Rice Stuffed Bell Peppers

Serves 4

Ingredients:

8 bell peppers, cored and seeded

1 1/2 cups rice, washed and drained

2 onions, chopped

1 tomato, chopped

fresh parsley, chopped

3 tbsp oil

1 tbsp paprika

Directions:

Heat the oil and sauté the onions for 2-3 minutes. Add the paprika, the washed and rinsed rice, the tomato, and season with salt and pepper. Add 1/2 cup of hot water and cook the rice until the water is absorbed. Stuff each pepper with the mixture using a spoon. Every pepper should be 3/4 full.

Arrange the peppers in a deep ovenproof dish and top up with warm water to half fill the dish. Cover and bake for about 20 minutes at 350 F. Uncover and cook for another 15 minutes until the peppers are well cooked. Serve on their own or with plain yogurt.

Bean Stuffed Bell Peppers

Serves 5

Ingredients:

10 dried red bell peppers

1 cup dried beans

1 onion

3 cloves garlic

2 tbsp flour

1 carrot

1 bunch of parsley

1/2 crushed walnuts

1 tsp paprika

salt, to taste

Directions:

Put the dried peppers in warm water and leave them for 1 hour.

Cook the beans.

Chop the carrot and the onion, sauté them and add them to the cooked beans. Add as well the finely chopped parsley and the walnuts. Stir the mixture to make it homogeneous.

Drain the peppers, then fill them with the mixture and place in a casserole, covering the pepper's openings with flour to seal them during the baking. Bake it for about 30 minutes at 350 F.

Monastery Stew

Serves 4

Ingredients:

3-4 potatoes, diced

2-3 tomatoes, diced

1-2 carrots, chopped

1-2 onions, finely chopped

1 cup small shallots, whole

1 celery rib, chopped

2 cups fresh mushrooms, chopped

1/2 cup black olives, pitted

1/4 cup rice

1/2 cup white wine

1/2 cup sunflower oil

1 bunch of parsley

1 tsp black pepper

1 tsp salt

Directions:

Sauté the finely chopped onions, carrots and celery in a little oil. Add the small onions, olives, mushrooms and black pepper and stir well. Pour over the wine and 1 cup of water, salt, cover and let simmer until tender.

After 15 minutes add the diced potatoes, the rice, and the tomatoes. Transfer everything into a casserole, sprinkle with parsley and bake for about 30 minutes at 350 F.

Potatoes Baked in Milk

Serves 5-6

Ingredients:

4-5 medium potatoes

1 cup milk

5 tbsp olive oil

1 tsp salt

1 tsp black pepper

1 tsp paprika

1 tsp savory

Directions:

Wash the potatoes, peel them and cut them in thin slices. Put in a large baking dish together with the milk, oil, salt, pepper, paprika and savory.

Combine everything very well. Bake for about 30 minutes at 350 F.

Potato and Zucchini Bake

Serves 6

Ingredients:

11/2 lb potatoes, peeled and sliced into rounds

5 zucchinis, sliced into rounds

2 onions, sliced into rounds

3 tomatoes, pureed

½ cup water

4 tbsp olive oil

1 tsp dry oregano

1/3 cup fresh parsley leaves, chopped

salt and black pepper, to taste

Directions:

Place the potatoes, zucchinis and onions in a large, shallow ovenproof baking dish. Pour over the the olive oil and pureed tomatoes. Add salt and freshly ground pepper to taste and toss the everything together. Add in the water.

Bake in the preheated to 350 F oven for an hour and stirring half way through.

New Potatoes with Herbs

Serves 4-5

Ingredients:

2 lbs small new potatoes

1 tbsp peppermint

2 oz butter

1 tbsp finely chopped parsley

1 tsp dried rosemary

1 tsp dried oregano

1 tbsp fresh dill

1 tsp salt

1 tsp black pepper

Directions:

Wash the young potatoes, cut them in halves if too big and put them in a baking dish.

Melt the butter and pour over the potatoes. Season with the herbs, salt and pepper. Bake for 30-40 minutes at 350 F

Feta Cheese Stuffed Zucchinis

Serves 5-6

Ingredients:

5-6 zucchinis

3.5 oz feta cheese, grated

3 eggs

1 onion, finely chopped

1/2 cup milk

3.5 oz butter

salt

Directions:

Halve the peeled zucchinis lengthwise, hollow and salt. Sauté the finely chopped onion in half of the butter. Combine half of the milk, grated feta cheese and 1 egg in a bowl.

Stuff the zucchinis with the mixture, arrange in a baking dish and pour over the remaining 2 eggs beaten with the rest of the milk. Bake for approximately 30 min in a preheated oven. A few minutes before the dish is ready fleck the remaining butter over the zucchinis.

Mediterranean Vegetable Casserole

Serves 4-5

Ingredients:

2 cups uncooked small pasta

1 small red onion, chopped

1/2 cup canned chickpea, drained

1/2 cup oil-packed sun-dried tomatoes, drained and thinly sliced

1/2 cup green olives, pitted and halved

1 can (8 ounces) tomato sauce

1 cup crumbled feta cheese

1/2 cup sour cream

2 tbsp fresh basil leaves, chopped

1 tsp dried oregano

1/2 tsp dried thyme

salt and black pepper, to taste

Directions:

Cook pasta according to package directions. In a large bowl, combine all remaining ingredients.

Drain pasta and toss with vegetable mixture. Transfer to baking dish coated with cooking spray. Bake, uncovered, at 375 F for 30-35 minutes or until heated through.

Baked Mediterranean Casserole with Tofu and Feta Cheese

Serves 4-5

Ingredients:

2 lbs small new potatoes, washed and halved

1/2 cup feta cheese, crumbled

1 cup spicy tofu pieces

3 cloves garlic, crushed

2 cups cherry or grape tomatoes

3 tbsp rosemary, chopped or minced

3 tbsp olive oil

1/2 cup Parmesan cheese

salt and pepper to taste

Directions:

Preheat the oven to 350 F. Put the sliced potatoes, garlic, olive oil, rosemary, salt and pepper in an oven proof baking dish and mix them all together well so that the potatoes are well coated.

Place in the oven and bake for 20 minutes then stir and add the tomatoes, tofu and feta cheese. Sprinkle with Parmesan cheese and cook for 15 minutes more.

Okra and Tomato Casserole

Serves 4-5

Ingredients:

1 lb okra, stem ends trimmed

4 large tomatoes, cut into wedges

3 garlic cloves, chopped

3 tbsp olive oil

1 tsp salt

black pepper, to taste

Directions:

In a large casserole, mix together trimmed okra, sliced tomatoes, the olive oil and the chopped garlic. Add salt and pepper and toss to combine.

Bake in e preheated to 400 F oven for 45 minutes until the okra is tender.

Zucchinis with Chickpeas and Rice

Serves 4

Prep time: 30 min

Ingredients:

3 zucchinis, peeled and diced

1 bunch green onions, finely chopped

2 medium tomatoes, diced

1/2 can chickpeas, drained

1/2 cup rice

1/2 cup black olives, pitted and halved

2 cups water

5 tbsp sunflower oil

1 tsp salt

1 tsp paprika

1 tsp black pepper

1/2 cup fresh dill, finely cut

Directions:

Sauté the onions in olive oil and a little water for 1-2 minutes or until soft.

Transfer the onions in a baking dish and add in zucchinis, chickpeas, tomatoes, olives, rice, salt, paprika, black pepper and water. Stir to combine well.

Cover with a lid or aluminum foil and bake at 350 F for 20 minutes, or until the rice is done.

Sprinkle with dill and serve.

FREE BONUS RECIPES:
15 Heartwarming Slow Cooker Soup Recipes Inspired by the Mediterranean Diet

Mediterranean Chickpea Soup

Serves 5-6

Ingredients:

1 can chickpeas, drained

a bunch of spring onions, finely cut

2 cloves garlic, crushed

1 can tomatoes, diced

4 cups vegetable broth

1/2 medium cabbage, cored and cut into 8 wedges

3 tbsp olive oil

1 bay leaf

½ tsp rosemary

½ cup freshly grated Parmesan cheese

Directions:

In a skillet, gently sauté onion and garlic in olive oil. Add to the slow cooker together with broth, chickpeas, tomatoes, bay leaf and rosemary.

Cook on high setting for 4 hours. Nestle cabbage into the soup, cover and cook until it is tender, about 20 minutes on high. Serve sprinkled with Parmesan cheese.

French Vegetable Soup

Serves 4-5

Ingredients:

1 leek, thinly sliced

1 large zucchini, peeled and diced

1 cup green beans, halved

2 large potatoes, peeled and cut into large chunks

1 medium fennel bulb, trimmed, cored, and cut into large chunks

2 garlic cloves, cut

4 cups vegetable broth

black pepper, to taste

4 tbsp freshly grated Parmesan cheese

Directions:

Combine all ingredients in slow cooker. Season with salt and pepper to taste. Cook on low for 6-10 hours or high for 2.5-3 hours.

Serve warm sprinkled with Parmesan cheese.

Minted Pea Soup

Serves 4

Ingredients:

1 onion, finely chopped

1 carrot, chopped

2 garlic cloves, finely chopped

4 cups vegetable broth

1/3 cup mint leaves

2 lb green peas, frozen

3 tbsp olive oil

1/4 cup yogurt, to serve

small mint leaves, to serve

Directions:

Heat oil in a skillet over medium-high heat and sauté onion and garlic for 2-3 minutes or until soft.

Add to a slow cooker together with the vegetable broth, mint, carrot and peas. Season with salt to taste. Cover and cook on low for 6-10 hours or high for 2.5-3 hours.

Blend in batches, until smooth. Return soup to slow cooker and cook for 10 minutes on low. Serve topped with yogurt and mint leaves.

Brown Lentil Soup

Serves 8-9

Ingredients:

2 cups brown lentils

2 onions, chopped

5-6 cloves garlic, peeled

3 medium carrots, chopped

2-3 medium tomatoes, ripe

6 cups water

1 ½ tsp paprika

1 tsp summer savory

Directions:

Add all ingredients into slow cooker. Cover and cook on low for 8 hours or high for 4 hours. Season with salt to taste and serve.

Moroccan Lentil Soup

Serves 8-9

Ingredients:

1 cup red lentils

1/2 cup canned chickpeas, drained

2 onions, chopped

2 cloves garlic, minced

1 cup canned tomatoes, chopped

1/2 cup canned white beans, drained

3 carrots, diced

3 celery ribs, diced

6 cups water

1 tsp ginger, grated

1 tsp ground cardamom

Directions:

Add all ingredients into slow cooker. Cover and cook on low for 8 hours or high for 4 hours. Season with salt to taste and puree half the soup in a food processor or blender. Return the pureed soup to the slow cooker, stir and serve.

Curried Lentil Soup

Serves 5-6

Ingredients:

1 cup dried lentils

1 large onion, finely cut

1 celery rib, chopped

1 large carrot, chopped

3 garlic cloves, chopped

1 can tomatoes, undrained

3 cups chicken broth

1 tbsp curry powder

1/2 tsp ground ginger

4 bacon slices, cooked and crumbled, to serve

Directions:

Combine all ingredients in slow cooker.

Cover and cook on low for 5-6 hours.

Blend soup to desired consistency, adding additional hot water to thin, if desired.

Serve topped with crumbled bacon.

Simple Black Bean Soup

Serves 5-6

Ingredients:

1 cup dried black beans

5 cups vegetable broth

1 large onion, chopped

1 red pepper, chopped

1 tsp sweet paprika

1 tbsp dried mint

2 bay leaves

1 serrano chile, finely chopped

1 tsp salt

4 tbsp fresh lime juice

1/2 cup chopped fresh cilantro

1 cup sour cream or yogurt, to serve

Directions:

Wash beans and soak them in enough water overnight.

In a slow cooker, combine the beans and all other ingredients except for the lime juice and cilantro. Cover and cook on low for 7-8 hours.

Add salt, lime juice and fresh cilantro.

Serve with a dollop of sour cream or yogurt.

Bean and Pasta Soup

Serves 6-7

Ingredients:

1 cup small pasta, cooked

1 cup canned white beans, rinsed and drained

2 medium carrots, cut

1 cup fresh spinach, torn

1 medium onion, chopped

1 celery rib, chopped

2 garlic cloves, crushed

3 cups water

1 cup canned tomatoes, diced and undrained

1 cup vegetable broth

½ tsp rosemary

½ tsp basil

salt and pepper, to taste

Directions:

Add all ingredients except pasta and spinach into slow cooker. Cover and cook on low for 6-7 hours or high for 4 hours. Add spinach and pasta about 30 minutes before soup is finished cooking.

Heartwarming Split Pea Soup

Serves 5-6

Ingredients:

1 lb dried green split peas, rinsed and drained

2 potatoes, peeled and diced

1 small onion, chopped

1 celery rib, chopped

1 carrot, chopped

2 garlic cloves, chopped

1 bay leaf

1 tsp black pepper

1/2 tsp salt

6 cups water

Grated feta cheese, to serve

Directions:

Combine all ingredients in slow cooker.

Cover and cook on low for 5-6 hours.

Discard bay leaf. Blend soup to desired consistency, adding additional hot water to thin, if desired.

Sprinkle grated feta cheese on top and serve with garlic or herb bread.

Minestrone

Serves 4-5

Ingredients:

¼ cabbage, chopped

2 carrots, chopped

1 celery rib, thinly sliced

1 small onion, chopped

2 garlic cloves, chopped

4 cups vegetable broth

1 cup canned tomatoes, diced, undrained

1 cup fresh spinach, torn

black pepper and salt, to taste

Directions:

Add all ingredients except spinach into slow cooker. Cover and cook on low for 6-7 hours or high for 4 hours.

Add spinach about 30 minutes before soup is finished cooking.

Slow Cooker Summer Garden Soup

Serves 4-5

Ingredients:

1 small onion, finely cut

2 carrots, chopped

1 zucchini, peeled and cubed

1 box frozen baby lima beans, thawed

1 celery rib, thinly sliced

2 garlic cloves, chopped

4 cups vegetable broth

1 can tomatoes, diced, undrained

1 medium yellow summer squash, cubed

1 cup uncooked small pasta

3-4 tbsp pesto

black pepper and salt, to taste

Directions:

Add all ingredients except zucchini, summer squash and pasta into slow cooker. Cover and cook on low for 6 hours or high for 4 hours.

Stir in pasta, zucchini and yellow squash. Cover; cook 1 hour longer or until vegetables are tender. Top individual servings with pesto.

Crock Pot Tomato Basil Soup

Serves: 5-6

Ingredients:

4 cups chopped fresh tomatoes or 27 oz can tomatoes

1/3 cup rice

3 cups water

1 large onion, diced

4 garlic cloves, minced

3 tbsp olive oil

1 tsp salt

1 tbsp dried basil

1 tbsp paprika

1 tsp sugar

½ bunch fresh parsley, to serve

Directions:

In a skillet, sauté onion and garlic for 2-3 minutes. When onions have softened, add them together with all other ingredients to the crock pot.

Cook on low for 5-7 hours, or on high for 3 1/2. Blend with an immersion blender and serve topped with fresh parsley.

Cheesy Cauliflower Soup

Serves 4-5

Ingredients:

1 large onion, finely cut

1 medium head cauliflower, chopped

2-3 garlic cloves, minced

4 cups vegetable broth

1 cup whole cream

1 cup cheddar cheese, grated

salt, to taste

fresh ground black pepper, to taste

Directions:

Put cauliflower, onion, garlic and vegetable broth in crock pot. Cover and cook on low for 4-6 hours. Blend in a blender.

Return to crockpot and blend in cream and cheese. Season with salt and pepper and stir to mix.

Creamy Artichoke Soup

Serves 4

Ingredients:

1 can artichoke hearts, drained

3 potatoes, peeled and cut into ½-inch pieces

1 small onion, finely cut

2 cloves garlic, crushed

3 cups vegetable broth

2 tbsp lemon juice

1 cup heavy cream

black pepper, to taste

Directions:

Combine the potatoes, onion, artichoke hearts, broth, lemon juice and black pepper in the slow cooker.

Cover and cook on low for 8-10 hours or on high for 4-5 hours or until the potatoes are tender.

Blend the soup in batches and return it to the slow cooker. Add the cream and continue to cook until heated 5-10 minutes more. Garnish with a swirl of cream or a sliver of artichoke.

Tomato Artichoke Soup

Serves 4

Ingredients:

1 can artichoke hearts, drained

1 can diced tomatoes, undrained

3 cups vegetable broth

1 small onion, chopped

2 cloves garlic, crushed

1 tbsp pesto

black pepper, to taste

Directions:

Combine all ingredients in the slow cooker.

Cover and cook on low for 8-10 hours or on high for 4-5 hours.

Blend the soup in batches and return it to the slow cooker. Season with salt and pepper to taste and serve.

About the Author

Vesela lives in Bulgaria with her family of six (including the Jack Russell Terrier). Her passion is going green in everyday life and she loves to prepare homemade cosmetic and beauty products for all her family and friends.

Vesela has been publishing her cookbooks for over a year now. If you want to see other healthy family recipes that she has published, together with some natural beauty books, you can check out her Author Page on Amazon.

Printed in Great Britain
by Amazon

14207550R00051